I0426221

April 2012

URGENT WARFIGHTER NEEDS

Opportunities Exist to Expedite Development and Fielding of Joint Capabilities

April 2012

URGENT WARFIGHTER NEEDS

Opportunities Exist to Expedite Development and Fielding of Joint Capabilities

Why GAO Did This Study

With the conflicts in Iraq and Afghanistan, DOD has had to accelerate efforts to field capabilities addressing urgent warfighter needs, including joint needs affecting more than one service. GAO was asked to assess (1) how quickly capabilities responding to joint urgent operational needs have been developed and fielded and (2) what key practices enabled executing organizations to overcome challenges. To do this, GAO studied a sample of joint urgent operational needs including all urgent needs over $100 million approved from April 2008 through December 2010 and a random selection of smaller urgent needs. GAO analyzed data on key events and issues in the development and fielding of solutions and met with service and DOD officials responsible for validating, assigning, and executing joint urgent needs.

What GAO Recommends

GAO recommends that DOD reduce the time spent on identifying and contracting for off-the-shelf solutions, devise methods for providing early funding to research laboratories and engineering centers, require that initiative decision memorandums be prepared for all initiatives, and require acquisition organizations to communicate with the Central Command and other combatant commands about plans for fielding capabilities. DOD concurred with these recommendations.

View GAO-12-385. For more information, contact Michael J. Sullivan at (202) 512-4163 or sullivanm@gao.gov.

What GAO Found

A majority of the initiatives GAO reviewed (26 of 30) met, or expected to meet, the Department of Defense's (DOD) expectation for fielding a capability in response to joint urgent operational needs within 2 years (see figure). However, performance in meeting schedule estimates varied, and more than half of the initiatives experienced schedule delays.

Time to Field Sampled Initiatives

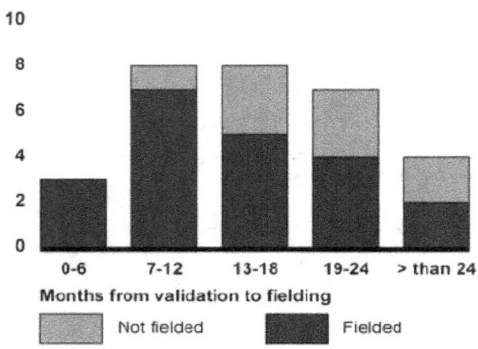

Number of sampled initiatives

Months from validation to fielding

Not fielded   Fielded

Source: GAO analysis of Department of Defense data.

Initiatives leveraged three types of solutions: (1) off-the-shelf products, (2) modifications of off-the-shelf items to add capabilities, and (3) products requiring technology development. Off-the-shelf solutions should be fielded the quickest because existing products are being bought. However, while off-the-shelf solutions were fielded quickly once a contract was awarded, it took longer than the two other types to identify, fund, and contract for off-the-shelf solutions. In addition to the program offices that manage traditional acquisition programs, initiatives were also managed by research laboratories and engineering centers, such as the Army Research Laboratory or the Naval Surface Warfare Center. Program offices fielded solutions faster, in part, because program offices are experienced in the full range of acquisition activities. Also, laboratories and engineering centers depended on funding provided by other organizations and delays in receiving this funding affected the start of some initiatives.

Acquisition organizations employed various practices to overcome challenges affecting fielding of capabilities within short time frames. For example, although these practices could affect the prices paid, shorter times were associated with using existing contracts, awarding contracts without agreeing on contract terms (prices), or awarding contracts without competition. U.S. Central Command officials stated that they were not aware of all initiatives underway or the expected schedule for fielding capabilities and this could affect planning activities. In some cases, initiative decision memorandums were prepared that documented schedule estimates but such memorandums are not required for all initiatives. Also, some organizations were proactive in communicating with U.S. Central Command and this facilitated a clearer understanding of requirements and plans for fielding initiatives, but regular communication is not required.

_____ United States Government Accountability Office

Contents

Abbreviations

CJCSI	Chairman of the Joint Chiefs of Staff Instruction
DOD	Department of Defense
JIEDDO	Joint Improvised Explosive Device Defeat Organization
Joint Staff	Office of the Chairman of the Joint Chiefs of Staff
JRAC	Joint Rapid Acquisition Cell
MRAP	Mine Resistant Ambush Protected Vehicle

United States Government Accountability Office
Washington, DC 20548

April 24, 2012

The Honorable Adam Smith
Ranking Member
Committee on Armed Services
House of Representatives

The Honorable Roscoe Bartlett
Chairman
The Honorable Silvestre Reyes
Ranking Member
Subcommittee on Tactical Air and Land Forces
Committee on Armed Services
House of Representatives

The dynamic nature of the enemy and tactical conditions encountered by forces in Iraq and Afghanistan have prompted the Department of Defense (DOD) to rapidly acquire and field new capabilities as quickly as possible in order to prevent mission failure or loss of life. Requests for newer capabilities have included technology to detect improvised explosive devices; sensors to provide increased situational awareness; and command and control equipment to warn personnel of hazardous areas and changing battlefield conditions. To accommodate the need for a rapid response, DOD has had to look beyond the traditional acquisition procedures and employ innovative techniques and methods to overcome institutional challenges and improve efficiencies. Requests that address the urgent needs of more than one service (joint urgent operational needs) are validated by the Office of the Chairman of the Joint Chiefs of Staff (Joint Staff) and then shepherded into the acquisition process by the Joint Rapid Acquisition Cell (JRAC).

DOD reports that funding the fulfillment of joint and service-specific urgent needs totaled at least $76.9 billion from fiscal years 2005 through 2010. In 2009, a Defense Science Board report identified DOD's funding processes as a major institutional barrier to rapidly developing and fielding new capability. Among other problems, our previous work has shown that DOD has had difficulty translating needs into programs.[1]

Urgent needs require a quick response time in order to deliver solutions that can reduce casualties and improve mission success. This requires that once urgent operational needs are validated, organizations are quickly tasked to develop and field needed capabilities. In response to your request, we assessed: 1) how quickly capabilities responding to joint urgent operational needs have been developed and fielded and 2) what practices enabled executing organizations to overcome challenges in the development and fielding of joint urgent need solutions.

To conduct this review, we selected a sample of 28 joint urgent operational needs from the population of 70 joint urgent needs that were validated from April 2008 to December 2010. We selected all 14 joint urgent needs with cost estimates greater than $100 million and randomly selected 14 joint urgent needs from the remaining 56 joint needs that had estimated costs of less than $100 million. Three joint urgent needs were dropped from the sample—in one case because the urgent need was terminated before it was assigned to a sponsor and in the other two cases because knowledgeable officials were not accessible. We encountered several instances in which multiple initiatives were pursued to address one joint urgent need. Each initiative was responsible for developing a capability and therefore the initiative became our unit of analysis. We reviewed a total of 45 initiatives addressing 25 joint urgent needs. For these initiatives, we collected and analyzed data on key events and issues in executing initiatives. We met with acquisition officials responsible for developing and fielding solutions, as well as officials from the Joint Staff, JRAC, the Joint Improvised Explosive Device Defeat Organization (JIEDDO), and other DOD officials responsible for validating and assigning joint urgent needs to the military services and agencies for leading joint efforts. Although the results presented in this report are limited to the initiatives we analyzed and cannot be projected to all urgent needs initiatives, they provide valuable insight on the length of time it takes to develop and field initiatives and the factors that affect development and fielding. (Additional details on our scope and

---

[1]GAO, *Warfighter Support: DOD's Urgent Needs Processes Need a More Comprehensive Approach and Evaluation for Potential Consolidation*, GAO-11-273 (Washington, D.C.: Mar. 1, 2011).

methodology are in app. I; the joint urgent needs we reviewed are identified in app. II.)

Because of the emphasis on quickly responding to urgent needs, we focused on the time taken to reach critical events such as tasking to an organization, awarding a contract, and initial fielding of a capability. Data were not available for all key events, in part because some initiatives were not yet complete. Figure 1 shows the number of initiatives analyzed based on availability of schedule data. This figure is used throughout the report to indicate the data being discussed.

Figure 1: Number of Initiatives Reviewed Based on Available Schedule Data

Total reviewed meeting **25 urgent needs**	45 initiatives
Schedule data available **From validation to contract award**	38 initiatives
Schedule data available **From validation to fielding**	30 initiatives
	21 fielded initiatives
	9 nonfielded initiatives

Source: GAO analysis of Department of Defense joint urgent need initiative sample.

We conducted this performance audit between January 2011 and April 2012 in accordance with generally accepted government auditing standards. Those standards require that we plan and perform the audit to obtain sufficient, appropriate evidence to provide a reasonable basis for our findings and conclusions based on our audit objectives. We believe that the evidence obtained provides a reasonable basis for our findings and conclusions based on our audit objectives.

Background

To be validated as a joint urgent operational need, a requirement must be joint in nature and, importantly, if not addressed immediately will seriously endanger personnel or pose a major threat to ongoing operations. DOD has taken a number of steps to provide urgently needed capabilities to the warfighter more quickly and to alleviate the challenges associated with the traditional acquisition process for acquiring capabilities.[2] The Office of the Secretary of Defense established JRAC in 2004 to help overcome institutional barriers and provide timely, effective support to meet the urgent materiel and logistics requirements that combatant commanders deem operationally critical. In July 2005, the Chairman of the Joint Chiefs of Staff issued Instruction 3470.01 to establish policy and procedures to facilitate the assessment, validation, sourcing, resourcing, and fielding of urgent combatant command needs considered as life- or combat mission-threatening, based on unforeseen requirements that must be resolved quickly. Although not addressed in the July 2005 instruction, DOD officials stated that a criterion for validation was the expectation that the capability gap could be addressed within 2 years. Subsequently, the Ike Skelton National Defense Authorization Act for Fiscal Year 2011 provided that the acquisition process for fielding capabilities in response to urgent operational needs is appropriate only for capabilities that can be fielded within a period of 2 to 24 months.

In June 2011, the Secretary of Defense established the Senior Integration Group to serve as DOD's single authority to prioritize solutions that can be fielded quickly and to direct actions to resolve issues associated with joint urgent needs, including requirements, resources, and acquisitions. In addition, the military services (Army, Navy, Air Force, and Marine Corps) have each established processes to address service-specific urgent and compelling warfighter needs.[3] Finally, in January 2012, the Chairman of the Joint Chiefs of Staff Instruction (CJCSI) 3170.01H was updated to integrate joint urgent operational needs as part of the joint capabilities

---

[2]DOD's framework for planning, executing, and funding its weapon programs relies on three decision-making systems—the Defense Acquisition System that relies on DOD Instruction 5000.02, *Operation of the Defense Acquisition System* (Dec. 8, 2008), to guide and manage the development and procurement of major weapon capabilities; the Joint Capabilities Integration and Development System to assess gaps and recommend solutions; and the Planning, Programming, Budgeting, and Execution process to allocate funding resources—all of which involve lengthy time frames, large budgets, and development efforts that can take decades to procure weapon systems.

[3]Headquarters, Department of the Army regulation 71-9, *Warfighting Capabilities Determination* (Dec. 28, 2009); Department of the Navy, *Navy Urgent Needs Process Implementation,* OPNAV 4000, ASN (RD&A) (July 26, 2007); Air Force Instruction 10-601, *Operational Capability Requirements Development,* July 12, 2010; and Marine Corps Order 3900.17, *The Marine Corps Urgent Needs Process and the Urgent Universal Need Statement* (Oct. 17, 2008).

GAO-12-385 Joint Urgent Needs

integration and development system to identify, assess, validate, and prioritize joint military capability requirements.[4]

In response to Section 804 of the Ike Skelton National Defense Authorization Act for Fiscal Year 2011, DOD is now in the process of assessing its policies and processes for managing both joint and service-specific urgent needs. This review is intended to establish policy that will be used to respond to urgent needs arising from future contingencies and will consider improvements to the acquisition process for rapid fielding of capabilities responding to urgent needs. In a February 2012 letter to the Chairmen of the Armed Services and Appropriations Committees, the Acting Under Secretary of Defense for Acquisition, Technology and Logistics stated that additional policy options were under development to address, among other elements, the need for more comprehensive policy to govern the acquisition of capabilities to satisfy urgent needs. DOD expects that the review of these policies will be complete by August 31, 2012.

The joint process begins when a need that is threatening to life or mission success is identified and a request is submitted to the commander of U.S. forces in a theater of operations, such as Iraq or Afghanistan. Once approved, the request is submitted to the combatant command headquarters, such as U.S. Central Command, for requests pertaining to Iraq or Afghanistan.[5] If endorsed at this level, the joint urgent need is then submitted to the Joint Staff where it is reviewed by a Functional Capabilities Board. The board is responsible for determining whether the urgent need addresses a capability gap that, if unmet, could threaten lives or the success of a combat mission. If the need meets these criteria, the board convenes a working group that collects additional information and makes recommendations for the review, including whether the Joint Staff Deputy Director for Requirements should validate the need. Once validated, the joint need is sent to JRAC who assigns a military service or agency as the sponsor. JIEDDO is generally the sponsor for joint urgent

---

[4]The CJCSI 3170.01H results in the cancellation of CJCSI 3170.01G, *Joint Capabilities Integration and Development System* (Mar. 1, 2009); CJCSI 3470.01, *Rapid Validation and Resourcing of Joint Urgent Operational Needs (JUONs) in the Year of Execution* (July 15, 2005).

[5]The U.S. Central Command is one of 10 combatant commands. It is headquartered at MacDill Air Force Base, Florida and its area of responsibility covers 20 countries, stretching from Afghanistan to Egypt and the Persian Gulf.

needs focused on countering improvised explosive devices. The sponsor is responsible for tasking executing organizations to lead the development and fielding of the capability, as well as providing oversight, guidance, and in most cases, funding.

The major events throughout the joint urgent needs life cycle are described in figure 2 for urgent needs originating from operations in Iraq and Afghanistan. While the joint urgent needs process begins when a request is submitted in theater, our analysis focused on the part of the process beginning at validation of the need and ending with the fielding of the first units of the capability in theater. From validation, the joint urgent needs process consists of five key events.

Figure 2: Steps in the Joint Urgent Operational Needs Process for Iraq and Afghanistan

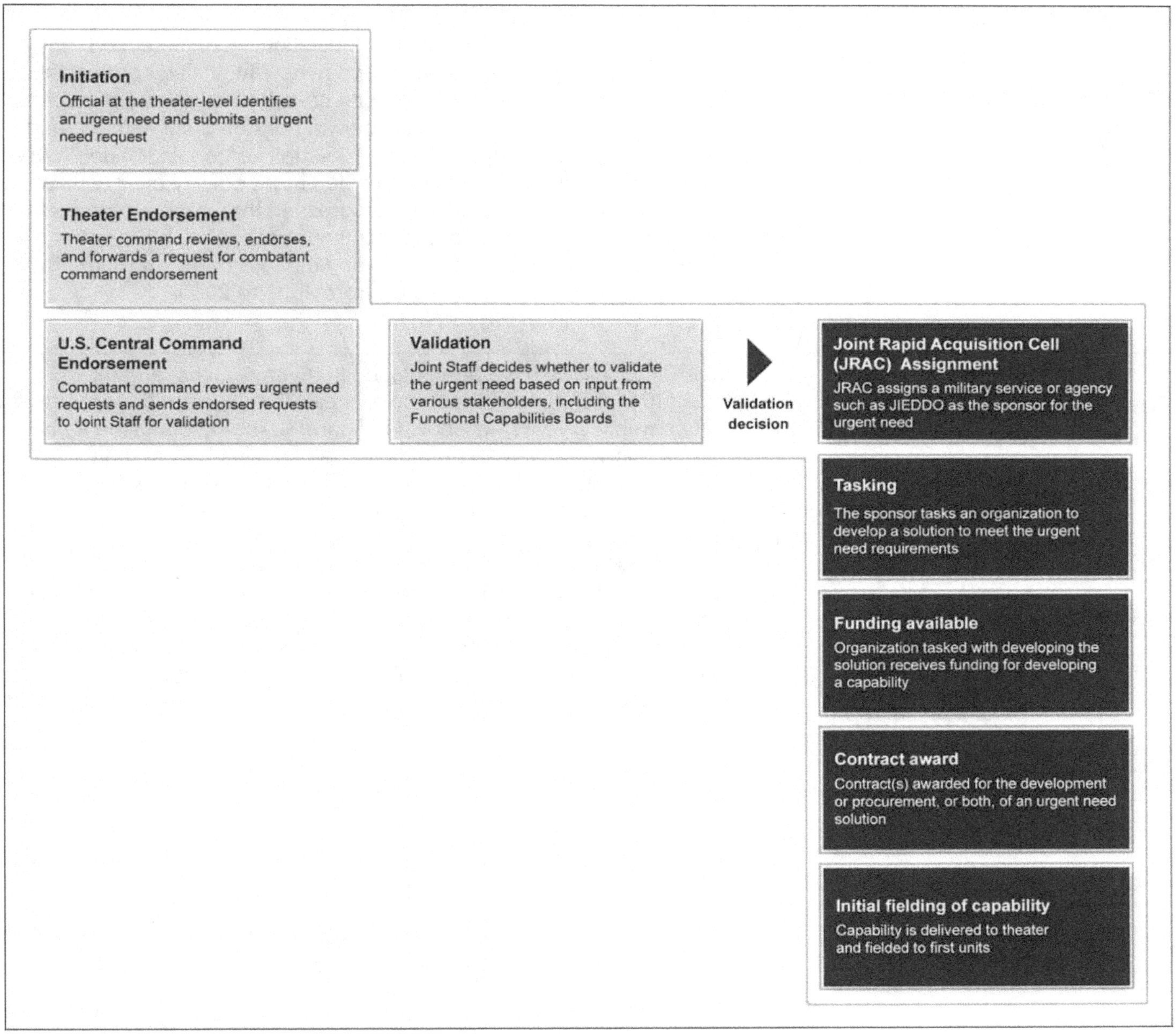

Initiation
Official at the theater-level identifies an urgent need and submits an urgent need request

Theater Endorsement
Theater command reviews, endorses, and forwards a request for combatant command endorsement

U.S. Central Command Endorsement
Combatant command reviews urgent need requests and sends endorsed requests to Joint Staff for validation

Validation
Joint Staff decides whether to validate the urgent need based on input from various stakeholders, including the Functional Capabilities Boards

 Validation decision

Joint Rapid Acquisition Cell (JRAC) Assignment
JRAC assigns a military service or agency such as JIEDDO as the sponsor for the urgent need

Tasking
The sponsor tasks an organization to develop a solution to meet the urgent need requirements

Funding available
Organization tasked with developing the solution receives funding for developing a capability

Contract award
Contract(s) awarded for the development or procurement, or both, of an urgent need solution

Initial fielding of capability
Capability is delivered to theater and fielded to first units

Source: GAO analysis of Department of Defense data

Initiatives Generally Fielded within 2 Years, but More Than Half Experienced Delays

Twenty-six of the 30 initiatives met, or expected to meet, DOD's expectation for fielding capabilities within 2 years from validation, but the remaining 4 initiatives took longer. Performance in meeting schedule estimates varied, and more than half of the initiatives experienced schedule delays. Most of the initiatives we reviewed, including all of those that met fielding estimates, used solutions based on buying commercial or government off-the-shelf items or modifying off-the-shelf items to add capabilities. Those based on buying off-the-shelf items took longer in the initial stages of the process, but were fielded more quickly after contract award. The rate at which an initiative progressed through the process also varied based on the type of organization responsible for executing the initiative and the sponsor. The median time to progress through the early stages of the process decreased from 2008 to 2010.

Most Initiatives Fielded or Are Expected to Field Capabilities within 2 Years

A number of initiatives have been fielded in a year or less, and most initiatives (26 of 30) met, or expected to meet, the expectation for fielding capabilities within 2 years, as shown in figure 3. The median time to initial fielding of a capability was 13 months for fielded initiatives and an estimated 19 months for initiatives not yet fielded. Overall, the 30 initiatives consisted of a range of urgent needs solutions, including improvised explosive device disruptors and detectors, wide-area surveillance systems, and Mine Resistant Ambush Protected (MRAP) vehicles. Nine initiatives had not been fielded at the time of our review. These nine initiatives ranged from systems that detect homemade explosives to aerostat balloons that provide persistent surveillance capability and to machine-based Afghani language translation capabilities.

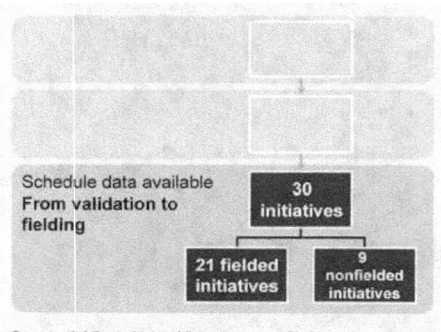

Schedule data available
From validation to fielding

30 initiatives

21 fielded initiatives

9 nonfielded initiatives

Source: GAO analysis of Department of Defense joint urgent need initiative sample.

Figure 3: Most Sampled Initiatives Were Fielded or Expected to Field within 24 Months

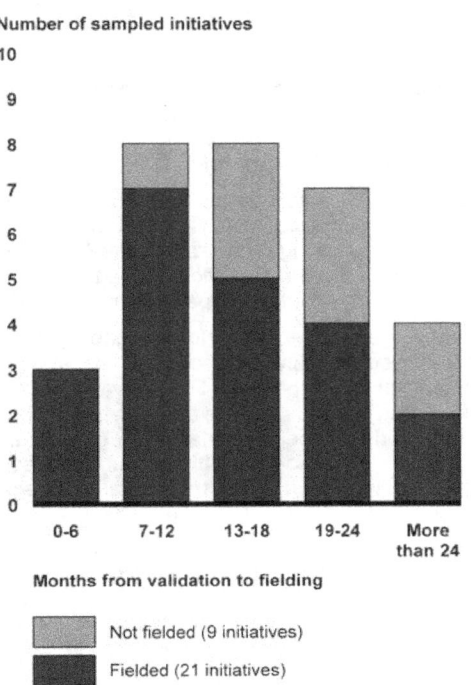

Number of sampled initiatives

Months from validation to fielding

Not fielded (9 initiatives)

Fielded (21 initiatives)

Source: GAO analysis of Department of Defense data.

Eleven initiatives took 12 months or less to reach initial fielding. For example, the MRAP Recovery Vehicle—a tow truck to retrieve disabled vehicles—reached initial fielding within 6 months of validation. According to program officials, this initiative benefited from existing relationships built during the development of other MRAP vehicles, as well as support from high-level stakeholders. One of the MRAP contractors anticipated the need for such a capability and developed the wrecker so that it was able to immediately respond to program office interest. Because of high-level support, approval for the acquisition was received even before the requirement was formally validated. In another example, the Persistent Ground Surveillance System, a system that provides surveillance and reconnaissance capability, reached initial fielding within 7 months because the program office had prior experience working in a rapid prototype environment. Program officials also said that earlier efforts enabled them to work with the vendor, become knowledgeable about the system, and work with contracting personnel who were very responsive to subsequent requests for the capability.

Four initiatives—two fielded and two not yet fielded—had actual or estimated fielding times of 27 months or more. Various factors contributed to the longer fielding times or estimates, depending on the initiative, as shown in table 1.

Table 1: Sampled Initiatives with Fielding Times Greater Than 24 Months

Initiative	Factors that contributed to fielding time
Data Classification and Processing System	According to program officials, this system met an urgent need for hardware and software that provided data access and functionality across intelligence domains. The capability was fielded in 28 months, 21 of which elapsed after the executing organization, the Army's Program Manager Distributed Common Ground System, awarded a contract. Officials said they spent considerable time educating the agency responsible for the network about the capability and working out data-sharing issues.
Entry Control Point in a Box	This initiative addressed an urgent need for a capability that could detect and defeat personnel- and vehicle-borne improvised explosive devices. Twenty-seven months elapsed from validation to fielding of a capability by the executing organization, Program Manager Improvised Explosive Device Defeat/Protect Force. Eighteen months passed after the organization received funding to fielding, during which time site surveys were conducted and specific capability needs identified, officials said. According to program officials, the requirement was modified after the funding decision was approved. Also, the change to reduce the original requirement had led the program manager to adjust contracts and procurement plans, causing delays. As a result, delivery to theater was delayed from 2010 to 2011.
Spectral Scientists	According to staff, the Naval Postgraduate School modified an existing curriculum to create a 1-year Master's degree to train experts who will work in the DOD and intelligence community to detect homemade explosive devices and materials. The estimated completion date of the training for the initial group of specialists is 28 months from validation. This initiative was one of several responding to the urgent need, and the academic institution was tasked 8 months after validation, when other efforts were already underway.
Handheld Biometric Solution	According to program officials, this initiative responded to an urgent need for improved biometric systems at bases in Afghanistan. Of the 28 months that elapsed from validation to the estimated fielding date, about half of the time occurred prior to contract award. Officials of the executing organization, Program Manager Biometrics Identity Management Agency, noted that the majority of delays they faced were related to the contracting process; in particular, the organization dealt with five different contracting officers prior to contract award. Once a contract was awarded, meeting the urgent need required hardware procurement as well as software development for biometric devices, officials said.

Source: GAO analysis of Department of Defense data.

Performance in meeting schedule estimates varied. Eleven of the sampled initiatives met, or were on track to meet, estimated fielding dates. However, 19 of the 30 sampled initiatives reported delays, and 12 of these initiatives exceeded their originally estimated fielding dates by at least 3 months, as illustrated in figure 4. Officials attributed the delays to some key issues that included the receipt of initial funding, awarding contracts, and conducting test activities.

GAO-12-385 Joint Urgent Needs

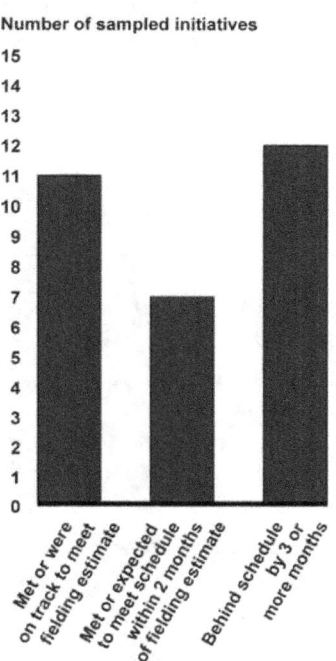

Figure 4: More Than Half of the Sampled Initiatives Experienced Delays

Number of sampled initiatives

Source: GAO analysis of Department of Defense data.

Off-the-Shelf Initiatives Were Slower Early in the Process Than Other Solution Types, but Were Fielded More Quickly after Contract Award

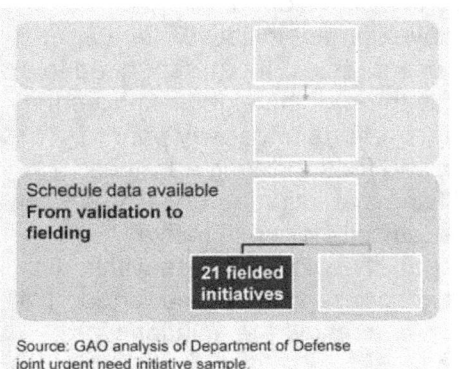

Schedule data available
From validation to fielding

21 fielded initiatives

Source: GAO analysis of Department of Defense joint urgent need initiative sample.

Initiatives that addressed joint urgent operational needs leveraged three types of solutions: (1) off-the-shelf products, (2) modifications of off-the-shelf items to add capabilities, and (3) products that required development of a technology. Off-the-shelf solutions should be fielded the quickest because they are focused on buying already-existing products. However, this was not the case for initiatives in our sample. Overall, off-the-shelf solutions in our sample tended to take somewhat longer to field than other solution types, a median time of 13.5 months compared to 12 months for modifications of off-the-shelf products and 11 months for technology development. Once a contract was awarded, off-the-shelf solutions were fielded quickly. However, as shown in figure 5, off-the-shelf solutions took longer in the early stages of the process. The median time to task, fund, and award a contract for off-the-shelf solutions was 9.5 months compared to 2 months for technology development solutions and 4 months for modified off-the-shelf solutions.

Figure 5: Off-the-Shelf Solutions Took Longer Initially but Were Delivered More Quickly after Contract Award for Sampled Initiatives

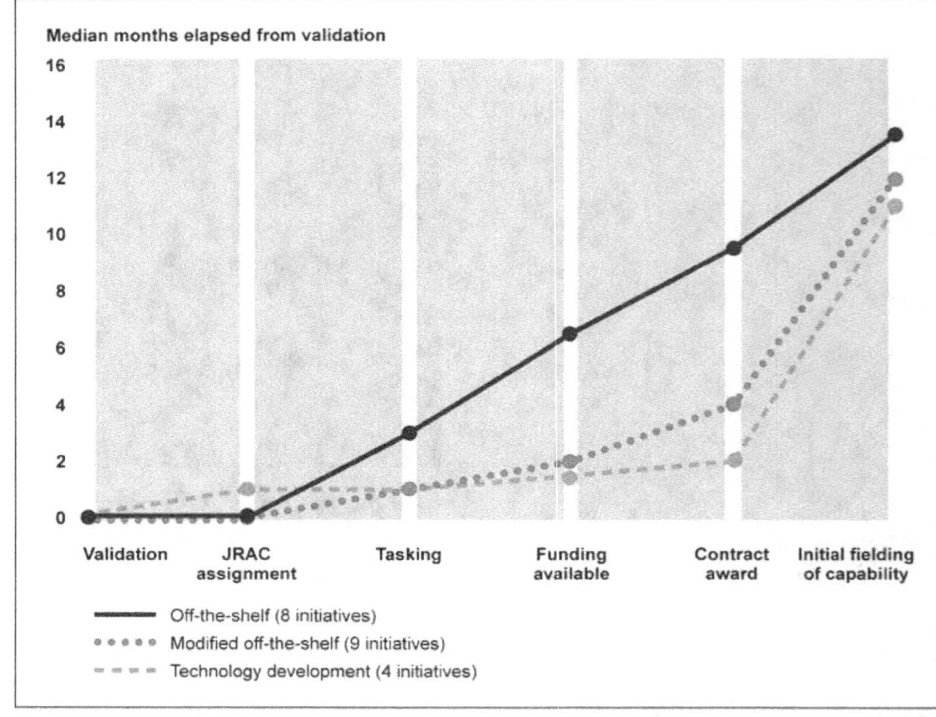

Source: GAO analysis of Department of Defense data.

Off-the-shelf solutions took longer during the early phases, in part, because they were less likely than other solution types to leverage ongoing efforts and thus required additional time to identify, fund, and contract for the solution. In contrast, other solution types—technology development and modifications of existing systems—leveraged ongoing efforts where solutions were at least partially developed. All 13 of the modified off-the-shelf and technology development initiatives leveraged efforts already underway before the sponsor tasked the urgent need to an acquisition organization. In contrast, only three of the eight initiatives that employed off-the-shelf solutions leveraged efforts underway prior to tasking. Leveraging ongoing efforts allowed for shorter time frames because it collapsed the time for identifying a solution and tasking an organization to execute it. For example, officials for an initiative developing a wide-area surveillance capability said they were within weeks of delivering the first sensors (in response to a service request) at the time the urgent need was validated. As a result, the solution was identified quickly and the initiative moved swiftly through the early stages of the process.

The experience of four initiatives further illustrated why off-the-shelf initiatives in our sample took longer than other solution types early in the joint urgent needs process. For these four initiatives, more than 9 months elapsed from validation to the receipt of funding. The reasons for these delays varied by initiative, as shown in table 2.

Table 2: Sampled Off-the-Shelf Initiatives Requiring at Least 9 Months Early in the Joint Urgent Needs Process

Initiative	Factors contributing to delays in early phases
Night and All-Weather Sniper Equipment	Twenty months elapsed before the executing organization, Space and Naval Warfare Systems Command, received funding for this initiative, which provided night and all-weather sniper equipment. An official for the command highlighted issues in gaining funding approval within JIEDDO, and the initiative experienced a delay of about 8 months between the tasking of the urgent need and the receipt of funding. An official explained that initial and subsequent requirements changes and modifications by the Army, Marine Corps, and Special Operations Command contributed to the delays.
Entry Control Point in a Box	This initiative was for an urgent need requiring a capability to detect and defeat personnel- and vehicle-borne improvised explosive devices. The program manager for this initiative said that preliminary work for site surveys of the forward operating bases in Afghanistan was required in order to determine the vehicle and pedestrian configurations. According to the program manager, 5 months had elapsed before the executing organization was tasked. In addition to the time involved with site surveys, other delays were associated with the time it took to manage multiple contracts in which competition was involved, and incorporating a requirement change from theater which needed to be resolved and agreed on by the military services. Also, a requirement change to the mission reduced the original requirement and required the program manager to adjust contracts and procurement plans, delaying the program. The delivery to theater was delayed from 2010 to 2011.
Unmanned Aerial System Resupply	This initiative met an urgent need request for an unmanned aerial system that could transport supplies to warfighters in areas where weather, terrain, and enemies posed risks, officials said. Although work on the capability had started by the time the urgent need was validated, 10 months passed before the program office was officially tasked to address the joint urgent need. According to DOD officials, the time elapsed during this period was attributable to delays in selecting a capability and securing funding.
Improvised Explosive Device Detector	The initiative addressed the need for a capability that could detect nonmetallic and buried improvised explosive devices. JIEDDO conducted tests of two potential solutions, including the Minehound and the Mini-Handheld Standoff Mine Detection System. The originally selected Mini-Handheld Standoff Mine Detection System failed to meet requirements. Minehound was tested in parallel but it also initially failed to meet requirements. The Army Research Laboratory was able to resolve the issues associated with Minehound but the Mini-Handheld Standoff Mine Detection System performance issues could not be resolved as quickly. Modifications to the system delayed testing and put the program behind schedule. These issues, in addition to JIEDDO's process of identifying and selecting a solution, contributed to the 10 months elapsed between tasking of the urgent need and the receipt of funding.

Source: GAO analysis of Department of Defense data.

After contract award, however, initiatives that required technology development or modification took longer to field as a result of technical challenges and testing delays. Off-the-shelf solutions relied on mature technologies and therefore could be fielded in a median time of 4 months after contract award. This compared to a median time of 8 months for initiatives modifying off-the-shelf products and 9 months for technology development efforts. Three of the four fielded initiatives that developed technology responded to the same urgent need for a wide-area surveillance capability. Officials working on these initiatives highlighted various issues that extended the fielding schedule subsequent to the awarding of a contract, including technical challenges and delays related to certification and accreditation of the solution.

Most of the fielded initiatives we reviewed, including all of those that met fielding dates, used solutions based on off-the-shelf items in response to joint urgent operational needs. Specifically, 17 of the 21 fielded initiatives either employed off-the-shelf products or modified off-the-shelf items. As figure 6 illustrates, the eight initiatives that met, or expected to meet, schedule estimates for fielding a capability leveraged off-the-shelf items or modified them to address the urgent need.

Figure 6: Sampled Initiatives Meeting Schedule Estimates Used Off-the-Shelf Solutions or Modified Off-the-Shelf Solutions

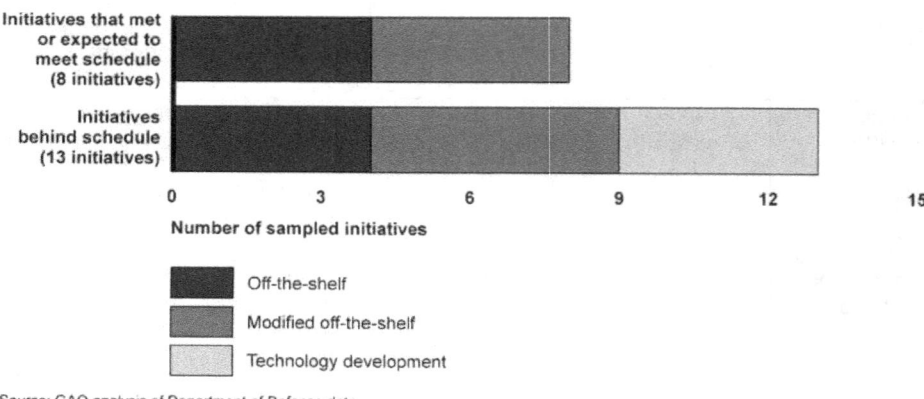

Source: GAO analysis of Department of Defense data.

Program Offices Delivered Capabilities Faster Than Other Organizations

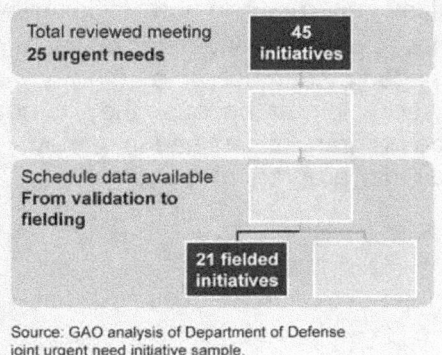

Source: GAO analysis of Department of Defense joint urgent need initiative sample.

Joint urgent needs are executed by a broader range of organizations than those typically responsible for managing acquisitions, as shown in figure 7. In addition to program offices that traditionally manage the acquisition and fielding of weapon systems, engineering centers and science and technology laboratories were tasked with executing initiatives. Engineering centers such as the Naval Surface Warfare Center and the Army Research, Development and Engineering Center typically provide support to the program offices that manage acquisition programs. Science and technology laboratories such as the Army Research Laboratory conduct technology development and research in the physical, engineering, and environmental sciences. In responding to urgent needs, both engineering centers and science and technology laboratories operate as reimbursable organizations, accepting project orders under which they get reimbursed for the costs of performing services, sharing knowledge, and conducting technical services.

Figure 7: Types of Organizations Executing Sample Initiatives

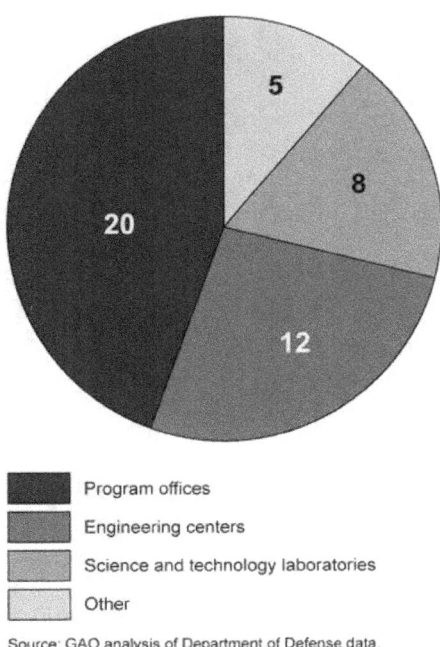

- Program offices
- Engineering centers
- Science and technology laboratories
- Other

Source: GAO analysis of Department of Defense data.

Program offices fielded capabilities faster than reimbursable organizations for the initiatives we reviewed, as shown in figure 8. The ability of program offices to field capabilities more quickly is partly explained by the expertise that these organizations have with the full range of acquisition activities, including developing test plans, accessing contract support, and planning for training and transportation. In addition, reimbursable organizations have a different funding environment than program offices in that they typically rely entirely on customer funding to perform work.[6] In contrast, program offices generally had greater flexibility in terms of their funding sources, which was particularly beneficial when funding delays occurred. Initiatives managed by reimbursable organizations took longer to field a capability, in part, because they do not have the same funding flexibilities as the program offices and they may need additional time to fully understand other program management processes.

---

[6]Reimbursable organizations provide products and services on a reimbursable basis, based on a customer-provider relationship between operating units and support organizations. Customers send funded orders to the providers such as Warfare Centers and Research Laboratories who furnish the services or products, pay for incurred expenses, and bill the customers, who in turn authorize payment.

Figure 8: Program Offices Fielded Solutions More Quickly Than Reimbursable Organizations for Sampled Initiatives

Median months elapsed from validation

| | Validation | JRAC assignment | Tasking | Funding available | Contract award | Initial fielding of capability |

- - - - Reimbursable organizations (12 initiatives)
——— Program offices (8 initiatives)

Source: GAO analysis of Department of Defense data.

Note: The number of initiatives is 20, instead of 21, because one of the organizations for which fielding data was available could not be categorized as either a program office or a reimbursable organization. We therefore removed the initiative from the analysis of schedule performance with respect to executing organization type.

JIEDDO Initiatives Took Longer to Reach Contract Award

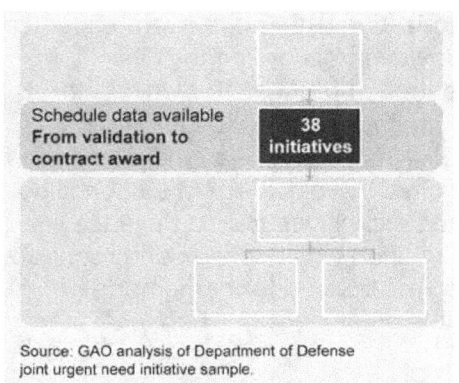

Source: GAO analysis of Department of Defense joint urgent need initiative sample.

The amount of time initiatives spent progressing through the urgent needs process, particularly before tasking to an organization, also differed depending on the sponsoring service or agency. As figure 9 shows, for the sampled initiatives, JIEDDO took longer than other sponsors to task an urgent need to an organization. The median amount of time sponsors, excluding JIEDDO, took to task initiatives to organizations was 1 month. In contrast, JIEDDO tasked its initiatives in a median time of 7 months.

Figure 9: JIEDDO Took Longer Than Other Sponsors to Reach Contract Award for the Sampled Initiatives

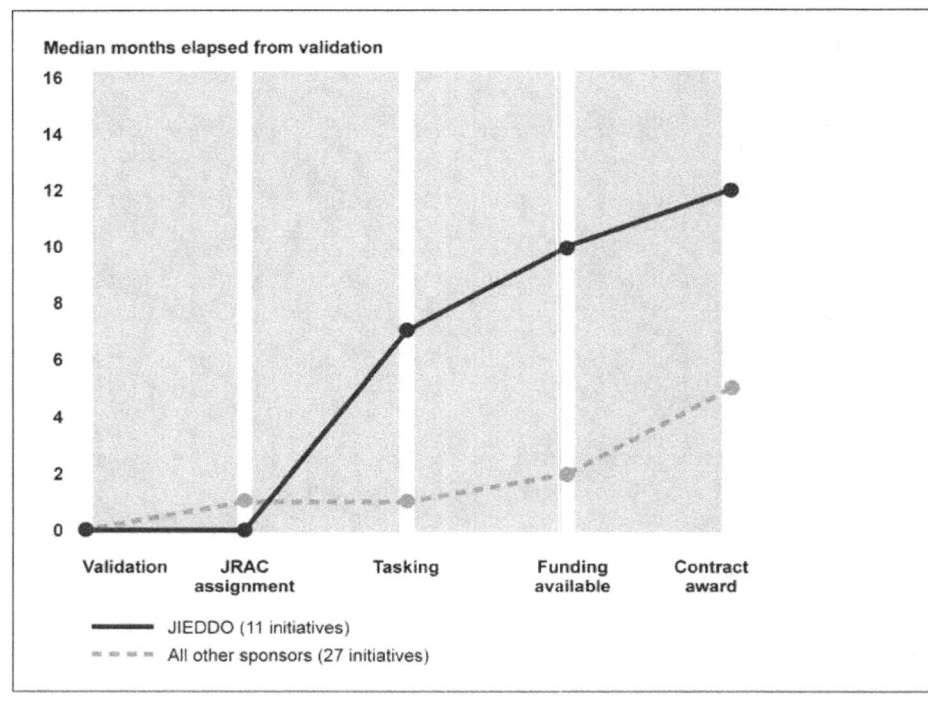

Note: Other services or agencies that led the initiatives we reviewed, besides JIEDDO, include the Air Force, the Marine Corps, the Army, the Navy, the United States Special Operations Command, the Defense Information Systems Agency, and the Intelligence, Surveillance, and Reconnaissance Task Force.

JIEDDO, however, had a more deliberate process for identifying and selecting a solution when one was uncertain, which helped explain why it took longer to task initiatives to an organization. Officials noted that the lead military service can quickly task urgent needs because an applicable solution, as well as the acquisition organization with the relevant expertise in developing it, is easily identifiable. However, according to DOD officials, JIEDDO often addresses urgent need requests for which the solution is ambiguous, therefore requiring greater effort to identify a capability and executing organization. For instance, one of the joint needs for which JIEDDO was the sponsor required development of a capability allowing warfighters to detect homemade explosives from a distance. According to officials, the urgent need solution was complex and required evaluation of various sensors and platforms tailored for homemade explosive detection. As a result, 7 months elapsed from when JRAC assigned the validated urgent need to JIEDDO to the point when the agency first tasked an organization with development of a solution. In the interim, JIEDDO worked to evaluate and identify potential capabilities to address the urgent need by forming a working group, writing a concept of operations, and completing a proof of concept. In the case of most other sponsors, the executing organization itself was responsible for activities such as developing a concept of operations and assessing solutions, officials said.

Initiatives Passed through Early Stages of the Process Faster in 2010 Than in 2008

Sampled initiatives validated in 2009 and 2010 were tasked and funded more quickly than initiatives validated in 2008, suggesting overall improvements in the earlier stages of the joint urgent needs process. Specifically, urgent needs validated in 2008 took 5 months longer than 2009 initiatives and 7 months longer than 2010 initiatives to be tasked and funded, as shown in figure 10.

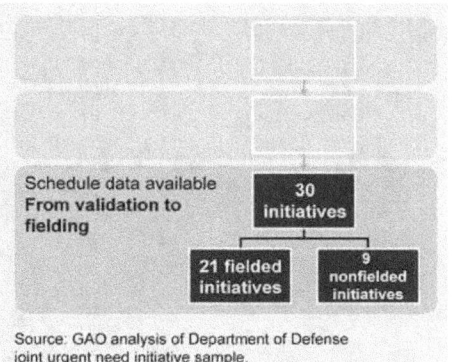

Source: GAO analysis of Department of Defense joint urgent need initiative sample.

Figure 10: Time to Funding Improved for Sampled Initiatives

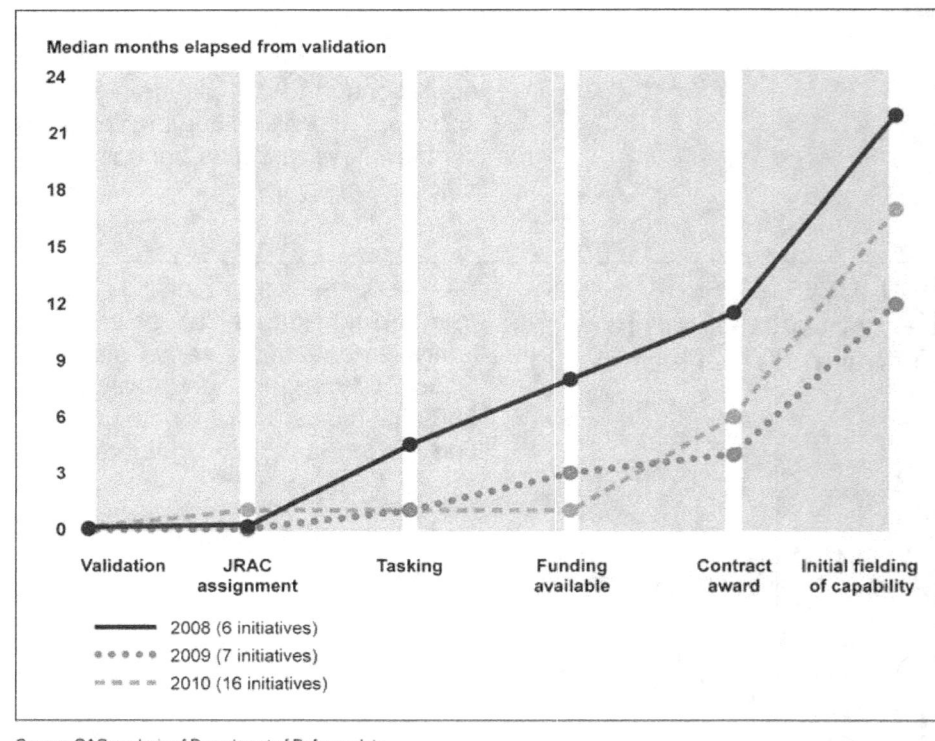

Source: GAO analysis of Department of Defense data.

Note: One initiative responded to a modification of an urgent need that was validated in 2011 and was not included in this analysis.

DOD officials cited the establishment of a senior group of officials to facilitate the joint urgent needs process as contributing to the reduction in the median time in which initiatives progressed through the joint urgent needs process since it was created. The deployment of additional forces to Afghanistan in the fall of 2009 led to an increase in demand for urgent need capabilities. Shortly after, in November 2009, DOD created the Counter-Improvised Explosive Device Senior Integration Group to provide oversight for all joint urgent operational needs related to counter-improvised explosive devices. DOD officials stated that the group has been renamed the Senior Integration Group, which is responsible for reviewing all validated joint urgent needs. The group, consisting of high-level DOD officials and agencies, meets every 3 weeks. According to DOD officials, the Senior Integration Group has helped increase oversight over the entire joint urgent operational needs process, and specifically accelerated the identification and allotment of funds to urgent need initiatives. In 2008, the median time initiatives spent from validation to the receipt of funding for the initiative was 9 months; however, initiatives validated in 2010 took no more than 1 month to receive funding during this time period.

Acquisition Organizations Employed Varying Methods to Overcome Challenges

In developing and fielding solutions addressing joint urgent operational needs, acquisition organizations faced common challenges that affected their ability to deliver capabilities as quickly as possible. These challenges included obtaining timely funding, addressing contracting requirements, and agreeing on testing that should be accomplished. Officials highlighted various practices—having early access to funds, receiving high-level support, using flexibilities in the contracting process, leveraging relationships, and communicating with the warfighter—that helped overcome challenges during solution development and fielding.

Early Access to Funding Speeds Execution

About half of the sampled initiatives received funding within 1 month of being tasked with an urgent need, but the remainder did not receive funding for 2 months or more, as illustrated in figure 11.

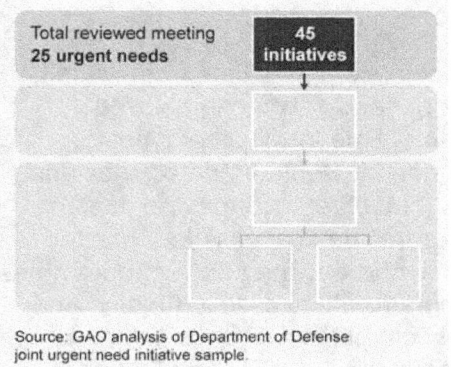

Source: GAO analysis of Department of Defense joint urgent need initiative sample.

Figure 11: About Half of the Sampled Initiatives Received Funding within 1 Month of Tasking

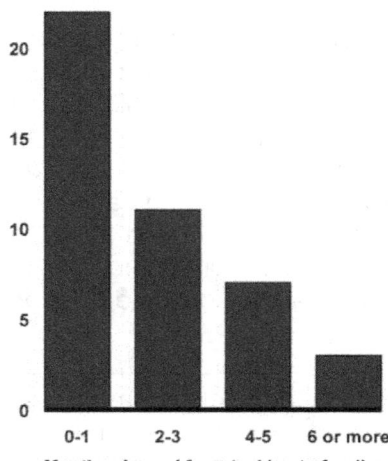

Number of sampled initiatives

Months elapsed from tasking to funding

Source: GAO analysis of Department of Defense data.

For initiatives within our sample, the median length of time from when a program office was tasked with an urgent need to when it received funding was 1 month; the median length of time for all other types of executing organizations, including engineering centers and science and technology laboratories, was 3 months. The difference may be due, in part, to the fact that some of these programs have access to budgeted funds. For example, according to agency officials, the MRAP program has an annual budget that provides the program with access to funding and requires that DOD notify congressional committees 10 days before it transfers these funds from the appropriation in the DOD and Full Year Continuing Appropriation Act, 2011. Although other program offices did not have such dedicated urgent needs funding, agency officials stated that, in some instances, they were able to leverage budgeted funds, as illustrated in the development of an unmanned cargo aircraft. This initiative managed by a Navy program office focused on developing and fielding an unmanned cargo capability to support forward operating bases in Afghanistan. The program office reported that it was able to reprogram funds from an alternate budget line when funding became a challenge. The Navy official said funding was important to begin early activities—such as developing an acquisition plan—particularly since the program had a 12-month deadline to deploy the capability.

Funding options were more limited for reimbursable organizations like engineering centers and science and technology laboratories. These types of organizations relied on customer funding and performed work in response to orders placed by other organizations, such as traditional program offices, that received appropriated funds. As a result, these organizations reported funding challenges more frequently than other organizations. Funding challenges were reported for 11 of 20 initiatives managed by engineering centers or science and technology laboratories. In contrast, 8 of the 25 remaining organizations in our sample reported funding challenges. The urgent need for a special purpose X-ray machine is one that experienced funding problems. The engineering center manager for this initiative said that the initiative experienced a 6-month delay due to 4 months in elapsed time to identify resources and 2 months for administrative problems associated with the transfer of customer funding at the end of the fiscal year.

While awaiting their major funding allotment early in the process, several organizations had access to a small amount of funding or were able to leverage existing resources to begin activities sooner. According to agency officials, JIEDDO, unlike JRAC or other sponsors, has the authority to provide up to $1 million in early or seed funding for administrative and programmatic start-up prior to the initiative decision memorandum authorizing funds for development or demonstrations.[7] Early funds can be used to support development of the acquisition strategy, test and evaluation strategy, and other programmatic documentation. Among the 45 initiatives in our sample, we identified eight instances where JIEDDO had provided executing organizations with early funding. In other instances, officials from executing organizations stated that they were able to leverage existing "in-house" resources to begin to research urgent needs solutions. However, officials noted that without funding, even staff time is limited and planning activities are constrained, particularly for reimbursable organizations.

Visibility by high-level stakeholders helped overcome funding challenges. Initiatives that had the attention of high-level stakeholders (such as the Secretary of Defense; the Senior Integration Group; JRAC; the Intelligence, Surveillance, and Reconnaissance Task Force; or JIEDDO)

---

[7]*Department of Defense JIEDDO, Joint Improvised Explosive Device Defeat Capability Approval and Acquisition Management Process*, JIEDDOI 5000.01 (Dec. 22, 2010).

experienced fewer delays in receiving their major funding allotment than those initiatives that did not have such visibility. In one example, a program office that was developing a wide-area surveillance capability had requested additional funding to accelerate ongoing efforts and meet the urgent need. When receipt of this funding was delayed, the Office of the Under Secretary of Defense for Acquisition, Technology and Logistics urged the Marine Corps to provide the program office with existing funds. This allowed the program office to continue developing the capability until its funding became available. Most notably, organizations that reported having high-level visibility among more than one of these stakeholders reported the fewest funding challenges. Executing organizations for only 2 of 11 initiatives that reported high-level visibility among more than one stakeholder also reported having funding challenges. In contrast, executing organizations for five of the six initiatives without high-level visibility reported having funding challenges. DOD officials noted that the establishment of the Senior Integration Group in 2011 has increased the visibility of high-level stakeholders into the joint urgent needs process and, more importantly, into urgent needs initiatives that may not normally receive such attention. DOD and program officials also stated that having high-level attention helped to prioritize and secure funding that otherwise could have been difficult.

Initiatives Leveraged Flexibility in the Contracting Process

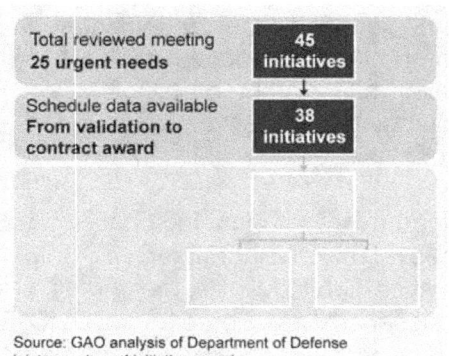

Source: GAO analysis of Department of Defense joint urgent need initiative sample.

In March 2010, the Under Secretary of Defense for Acquisition, Technology and Logistics issued a memorandum reinforcing urgent needs as DOD's highest priority and encouraging the acquisition community to use all available tools and authorities—including contracting tools and authorities—to develop and field capabilities more quickly. Initiatives we reviewed commonly used one or more contracting tools, including use of existing contracts, undefinitized (unpriced) contracts, and sole-source contracts.

Within our sample, 24 of the 38 initiatives leveraged existing contracts. As illustrated in figure 12, the median time to contract award was 6 months shorter for initiatives that used existing contracts.

Figure 12: Time to Contract Award Was Shorter for Sampled Initiatives That Used Existing Contracts

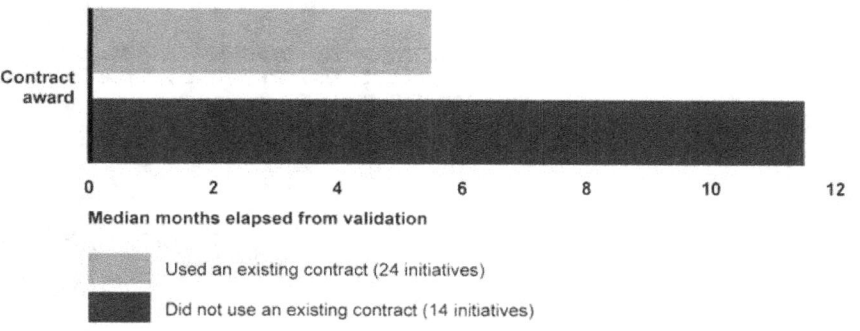

Median months elapsed from validation

Used an existing contract (24 initiatives)

Did not use an existing contract (14 initiatives)

Source: GAO analysis of Department of Defense data.

A program manager noted that using existing contracts was advantageous because the time traditionally taken to award a contract can exceed 6 months, at least 25 percent of an executing organization's schedule if it is trying to field a capability in less than 2 years. Another program official said that the use of existing contracts allowed the program to save time in acquiring needed materials, parts, and equipment since competing and awarding a new contract would have added time to the overall effort.

For initiatives that used an undefinitized contract—a contract action allowing contractors to begin work before reaching a final agreement on contract terms, such as price—the median time to reach contract award was 5 months shorter than those that did not, as shown in figure 13. As we have previously reported, when a requirement needs to be met quickly and there is insufficient time to use traditional contracting vehicles, defense regulations permit the use of an undefinitized contract action.[8] These can be quickly initiated, but at a later date, the contract's final price and other terms must be agreed upon by the contractor and government, a process known as definitizing the contract. The use of these contracting vehicles increases the risk to the government until the contract has been definitized. The MRAP program used undefinitized contracts for the three initiatives we reviewed—the MRAP All-Terrain Vehicle, the MRAP

---

[8]GAO, *Defense Contracting: DOD Has Enhanced Insight into Undefinitized Contract Action Use, but Management at Local Commands Needs Improvement*, GAO-10-299, (Washington, D.C.: Jan. 28, 2010).

GAO-12-385 Joint Urgent Needs

Recovery Vehicle, and the MRAP All-Terrain Ambulance. This allowed the contractors to begin work immediately to meet aggressive schedule targets while providing greater time to negotiate firm-fixed-price contracts.

Figure 13: Time to Contract Award Was Shorter for Sampled Initiatives That Used Undefinitized Contracts

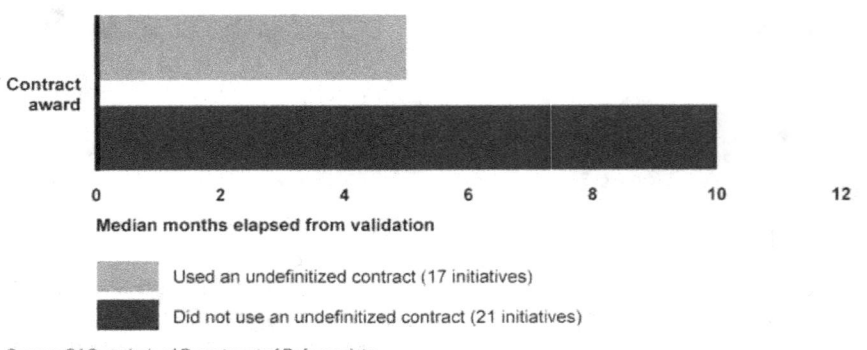

Median months elapsed from validation

Used an undefinitized contract (17 initiatives)

Did not use an undefinitized contract (21 initiatives)

Source: GAO analysis of Department of Defense data.

Executing organizations for 30 initiatives in our sample reported that they did not compete their contracts, and instead relied upon sole-source contracts. Program officials reported that they used the unusual and compelling urgency exception to full and open competition under FAR 6.302-2 associated with urgent operational needs to justify using sole-source contracts. As illustrated in figure 14, when contracts were competed, initiatives took more time to reach contract award than those that awarded sole-source contracts, although the reliance on sole-source contracts may affect the price the government pays. In the case of the MRAP program, however, officials relied on competition to incentivize contractors to invest in and develop alternative solutions. Particularly noteworthy was a contractor proposal to use underbody armor that addressed the need for greater protection for MRAP All-Terrain Vehicles; the solution was ultimately added to MRAP vehicles already in use, as well as those in production.

Figure 14: Time to Contract Award Was Shorter for Sampled Initiatives That Did Not Compete a Contract

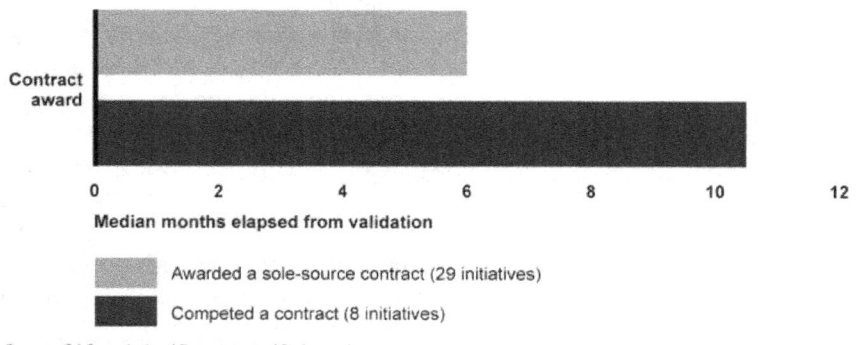

Contract award

Median months elapsed from validation

Awarded a sole-source contract (29 initiatives)

Competed a contract (8 initiatives)

Source: GAO analysis of Department of Defense data.

Note: One executing organization leveraged existing contracts but competed its contracts prior to being tasked and did not award other contracts; we considered its previous competition as not applicable to our review. We therefore removed this initiative from the analysis of schedule performance with respect to the use of competed contracts.

Leveraging Relationships Helped to Address Testing and Logistical Challenges

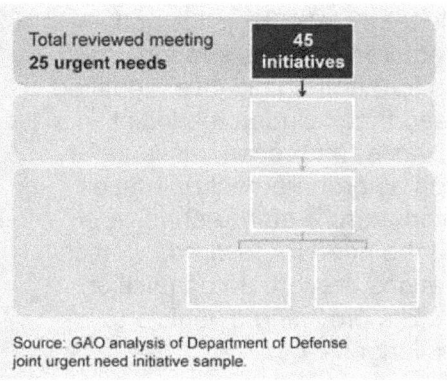

Source: GAO analysis of Department of Defense joint urgent need initiative sample.

Cooperative relationships with supporting organizations, such as those in the test and logistics communities, enabled some initiatives to overcome the difficulties associated with fielding capabilities quickly. Program officials stated that approaching the test community early and establishing working relationships with these organizations helped to make testing more efficient. Officials from executing organizations noted that testing performed on typical acquisition programs could not necessarily be completed within rapid time frames. In one example, the testing community requested 3-4 months to conduct tests on a capability, but the schedule only allowed 8 weeks for testing. Officials stated that an organization needs to involve the testing community early in the process to create a feasible test strategy. In another case, officials stated that the testing community was extremely cooperative and designed a test strategy based on discussions that were held early in development.

Some officials told us that once the organization completed development of the capability, they still faced challenges in obtaining approval to deliver the capability to theater. According to agency officials, several programs were required to obtain safety certification prior to deployment to theater and some executing organizations experienced delays in certification and accreditation of solutions.[9] For instance, officials from one initiative noted that 3 months passed after they had shipped a capability to Afghanistan while it received various forms of accreditation for the system's components, such as the ground station, network, and aircraft. This delay contributed to the 11 months spent from the time a contract was awarded to when a fully operational capability was fielded.

Logistical challenges were also problematic, according to officials, especially when their organization was not typically responsible for shipping capabilities into theater. Organizations anticipated and overcame logistics challenges by adapting the capability to facilitate shipping or by partnering with other DOD agencies for transporting materials. For example, one executing organization had special shipping requirements for materials requiring cooled storage while in transit. Instead of developing this capability on its own, the organization leveraged the experience of an Army agency that had the requisite logistics experience and knowledge. Officials for some initiatives stated that a list of best practices, or a one-page checklist with requirements and security information, would have made it easier for organizations to plan for these tasks and avoid having to figure it out on their own.

Testing and other challenges were at times discussed in acquisition strategies. For example, the acquisition strategy for the MRAP program discussed the level of testing that would take place, logistics and maintenance that would be provided, required facilities support, and training for personnel. Acquisition plans for another initiative identified important aspects of the joint urgent need that included the initiative's focus on increasing intelligence, surveillance, and reconnaissance capabilities, and other expectations such as procurement quantities, contractor support for procurement of commercial off-the-shelf components and materials, testing, and the need for tailored logistics support. JIEDDO requires that organizations prepare an acquisition strategy within 30 days of tasking, therefore providing a vehicle to address testing, logistics, and other challenges.

---

[9]Defense officials note that required safety documentation varies among the services and may take the form of a Safety Confirmation (created by a services testing capability) or Safety Recommendation.

Communication with Combatant Command During Solution Development Improved Expectations

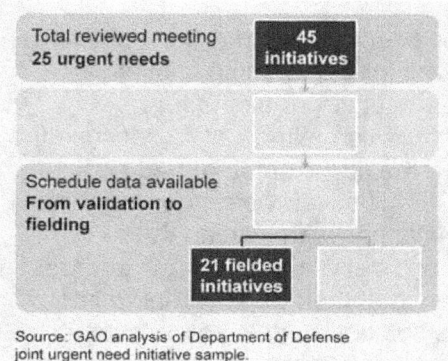

Source: GAO analysis of Department of Defense joint urgent need initiative sample.

Officials we spoke with said that communication throughout the joint urgent needs process—particularly between the acquisition community and the combatant command officials in Iraq and Afghanistan and at headquarters—aided in overcoming challenges related to the development and fielding of solutions. While the Joint Staff worked to define and clarify urgent needs requirements during validation, officials for 16 of the 45 initiatives in our sample stated that they had to work with U.S. Central Command officials in theater and at headquarters to further develop the requirements after they were tasked with the urgent need. The median time to initial fielding of a capability was over 8 months shorter for initiatives where officials worked with U.S. Central Command on requirements, as illustrated in figure 15.

Figure 15: Shorter Time to Initial Fielding Associated with U.S. Central Command Involvement in Refining Requirements for Sampled Initiatives

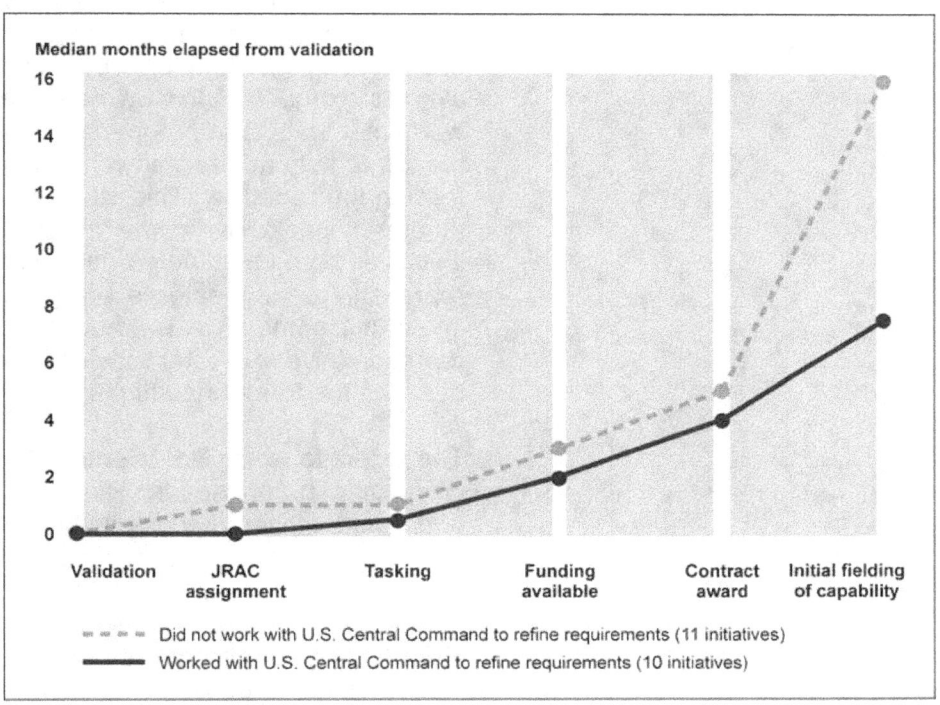

Source: GAO analysis of Department of Defense data.

Officials noted that it is important that urgent needs statements allow some flexibility for developing solutions so that acquisition organizations can make use of all available technologies to meet the warfighter's needs. In some instances, communication that began with requirements continued and supported fielding of the capability. For example, officials developing a capability to detect improvised explosive devices worked with officials in Afghanistan to clarify overly prescriptive requirements. Program officials noted that strong communication between the program and the warfighter was one of the most important factors that allowed their organization to field a solution within 14 months.

Officials also stated that communication with officials in theater before and after fielding a solution was important for overcoming challenges related to integrating the capability into the unit. For example, when solutions arrived in theater, problems could sometimes arise because the receiving warfighter unit was not always the same unit that had originally requested the capability. For 15 of the 45 initiatives we reviewed, officials reported that they had encountered challenges with fielding their capability due to units that rotated into and out of theater. They addressed this by contacting commanders in advance of their deployment to inform them of the fielding of the urgent needs solution and, in some instances, offered training to their unit. In many instances, a representative from the executing organization would also be in theater to assist receiving warfighter units. The program manager from one organization traveled to theater to help address any challenges associated with unit rotation and fielding the capability. This official emphasized that this presence in theater helped to overcome any challenges. While officials for 31 initiatives noted that their organization had, or planned to have, a representative in theater to aid in the fielding and integration of a solution into a unit, some officials noted that it was preferable to have a military representative in theater rather than a civilian employee or contractor because the former had higher visibility among the units.

The extent to which U.S. Central Command has knowledge of the progress of urgent needs initiatives depends, in large part, on the initiative of program officials in communicating such information. Officials at U.S. Central Command headquarters stated that they were not always aware of what solutions were being developed in response to joint urgent needs or of the progress being made by executing organizations. JRAC and JIEDDO largely rely on three databases to track urgent needs initiatives and document progress.[10] In these databases, information on specific

---

[10]Databases include the U.S. Central Command Requirements Information Manager database, the JIEDDO Enterprise Management System, and the Joint Staff's Knowledge Management/Decision Support tool.

GAO-12-385 Joint Urgent Needs

joint urgent needs, particularly those met by multiple initiatives, was often unclear or incomplete, making it difficult to identify the initiatives implemented in response to an urgent need. For example, not every sponsor or executing organization provided a point of contact for its initiative. JRAC officials explained that they solicit updates from executing organizations and provide these updates to U.S. Central Command and other groups—such as the Senior Integration Group—upon request. Inconsistent documentation presented challenges in tracking the progress of individual initiatives, as well as identifying points of contact for the organizations responsible for meeting urgent needs.

Problems cited by U.S. Central Command officials in identifying what initiatives were being developed in response to joint urgent needs were consistent with difficulties we encountered in identifying initiatives responding to the joint urgent needs in our sample. Officials from the Joint Staff, JRAC, and JIEDDO compiled a list of initiatives that responded to the joint urgent needs in our sample. For the urgent need addressing personnel- and vehicle-borne improvised explosive devices, additional initiatives were identified later. In another case—the urgent need addressing wide-area surveillance—officials identified additional initiatives that had not been identified previously.

Schedule estimates were not consistently available in databases used by U.S. Central Command, JRAC, and JIEDDO. Schedule plans were at times documented for meeting the joint urgent need more generally, but estimates of when a specific initiative would be fielded were often unclear or undocumented. Executing organizations for many initiatives (25 of 45) estimated initial fielding dates after being tasked with the joint urgent need, but not all organizations or sponsors formally documented schedule estimates. In many instances, estimated fielding dates were communicated in briefing slides or through informal means, such as e-mails.

For some initiatives, schedule estimates and expectations were documented and communicated in an initiative decision memorandum. In particular, an initiative decision memorandum was prepared for several JIEDDO-sponsored initiatives, and JIEDDO currently requires that an initiative decision memorandum be prepared for all JIEDDO-sponsored initiatives; however, there is no requirement that applies to all initiatives. The decision memorandums we reviewed generally included an estimated schedule for fielding the capability and called for preparing an acquisition strategy. Acquisition strategies we reviewed identified testing, logistics, and other resources needed to support the development and fielding of the capability and, according to officials, facilitated better planning and disciplined management. Defense officials noted that the initiative decision memorandum includes other important information such as cost and funding estimates, schedule of funding, appropriation totals, entry/exit criteria, and manpower implications. Furthermore, they stated that the document captures performance and schedule changes, establishes a formal agreement between the program manager and JIEDDO, and documents the initiative's life cycle from cradle to grave.

Officials at U.S. Central Command stated that having better communication during development of a solution could help facilitate planning activities and operational decisions that affect the warfighter. JRAC and JIEDDO officials stated that although not required, they see regular communication with the combatant command as important for all initiatives.

Conclusions

As DOD puts in place a policy for responding to future contingencies, it is important to understand what worked well and correct what did not work well in responding to urgent needs in Iraq and Afghanistan. Several practices have potential for facilitating a quick response to warfighter needs. Off-the-shelf solutions should be fielded quickly, but doing so requires reducing the time to decide on a solution, make funding available, and award a contract. Creating and leveraging the enablers—early funding particularly for reimbursable organizations, use of authorities to expedite the award of contracts, early involvement of stakeholders including the warfighter—will help reduce response time. Communicating with combatant command officials in theater and at headquarters about requirements as well as challenges in integrating a capability into warfighting units supported effective fielding, but there is no requirement that this communication take place. Clearly communicating what initiatives are being undertaken in response to urgent needs is important to those who plan and make decisions about theater operations. Initiative decision memorandums aided in communicating schedule expectations for JIEDDO initiatives, and in some instances acquisition strategies communicated risks and identified testing, logistical, and other resources that needed to be brought to bear during development and fielding of joint need solutions. But, there is no requirement that an initiative decision memorandum be prepared for all initiatives.

Recommendations for Executive Action

To improve the process for responding to joint urgent operational needs, we recommend that the Secretary of Defense take the following four actions:

- Expedite fielding of off-the-shelf solutions by reducing the time it takes to identify the solution and award a contract.
- Devise methods for providing early funding to reimbursable organizations tasked to execute joint urgent needs.
- Require acquisition organizations to communicate with the combatant commands, such as Central Command, regularly about progress in executing initiatives and plans for fielding capabilities.
- Require that an initiative decision memorandum be developed for all initiatives that identifies the acquisition organization responsible for the initiative, schedule estimates, and expectations for acquisition strategies.

Agency Comments and Our Evaluation

DOD provided written comments on a draft of this report. DOD concurred with all four of our recommendations, saying that it would address these recommendations as part of the assessment required by section 804 of the Ike Skelton National Defense Authorization Act for Fiscal Year 2011. DOD also provided technical comments that we incorporated in the final report. Their comments can be found in appendix III of this report.

We are sending copies of this report to the Secretary of Defense; the Secretaries of the Air Force, Army, and Navy; and the commanders for the Special Operations Command and the U.S. Central Command. The report also is available at no charge on the GAO website at http://www.gao.gov.

If you or your staff have any questions concerning this report, please contact me at (202) 512-4841 or sullivanm@gao.gov. Contact points for our Offices of Congressional Relations and Public Affairs may be found on the last page of this report. Staff members making key contributions to this report are listed in appendix IV.

Michael J. Sullivan
Director
Acquisition and Sourcing Management

Appendix I: Scope and Methodology

To review how the Department of Defense (DOD) has responded to urgent needs, we identified 70 joint urgent operational needs that were validated from April 1, 2008, to December 31, 2010. To create our nongeneralizable sample of initiatives to review, we selected all 14 joint urgent needs with cost estimates greater than $100 million and randomly selected 7 counter-improvised explosive device urgent needs and 7 other urgent needs from the remaining 56 urgent needs with cost estimates less than $100 million, as illustrated in figure 16.

Figure 16: Sample Joint Urgent Operational Needs Selected for Review

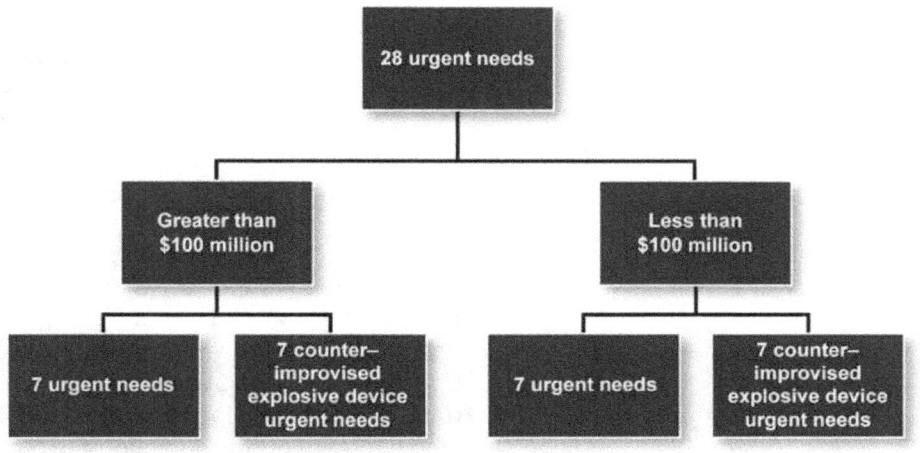

Source: GAO presentation of Department of Defense data

Three joint urgent needs were dropped from the sample—in one case because the urgent need was terminated before it was assigned to a sponsor and in the other two cases because knowledgeable officials were not accessible. We encountered several instances in which multiple initiatives were pursued to address one joint urgent need. As a result, we reviewed a total of 45 initiatives addressing 25 joint urgent needs. We collected the dates at which each initiative reached key events in the joint urgent needs process, including: urgent need validation, assignment to a sponsor, tasking to an executing organization, receipt of major funding allotment, first contract award or modification, and initial fielding of the capability. Moreover, the data available on initiatives varied, affecting the number of initiatives included in specific analyses, as shown in figure 17.

Figure 17: Number of Initiatives Reviewed Based on Available Schedule Data

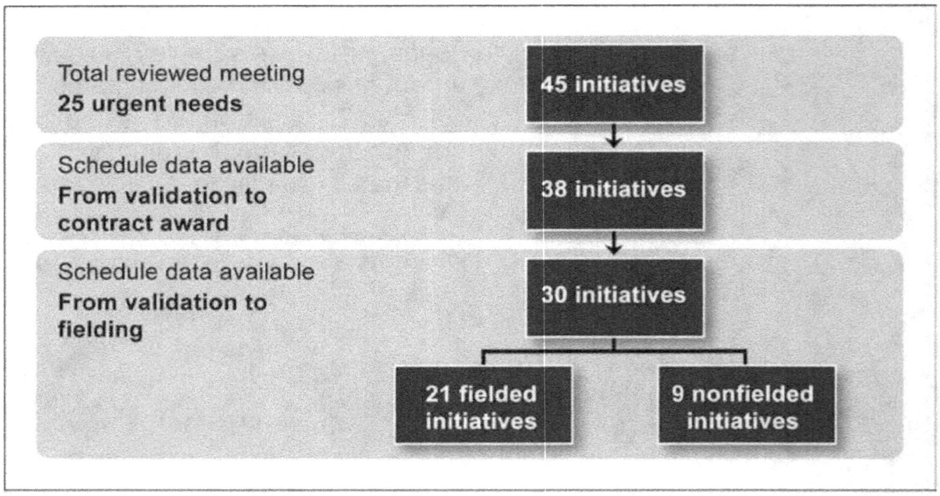

Source: GAO analysis of Department of Defense joint urgent need initiative sample.

To determine how quickly executing organizations developed and fielded capabilities in response to joint urgent operational needs, we assessed the extent to which executing organizations met the expectation to field urgent capabilities within 2 years. We reviewed the date on which the urgent need was validated, and identified either the actual or estimated date for initial fielding of a capability. We also assessed the extent to which executing organizations met their own schedule estimates by collecting and reviewing their first estimate for fielding the capability and their actual fielding date or most current estimate. We examined the time initiatives with certain characteristics took to field capabilities. We analyzed characteristics on each initiative including: the year the urgent need was validated; the sponsor; the type of executing organization tasked with the urgent need; whether the executing organization was working on a similar capability; and the type of solution. To assess the reliability of our data for this review, we compared information communicated by officials with initiative documentation, such as decision memorandums, briefing slides, and urgent need requests. We also reviewed information available in the three databases DOD uses to track joint urgent needs—the U.S. Central Command Requirements Information Manager, which is maintained by U.S. Central Command; the Knowledge Management/Decision Support tool, which is maintained by the Office of the Chairman of the Joint Chiefs of Staff; and the Joint Improvised Explosive Device Defeat Organization (JIEDDO) Enterprise Management System, which is maintained by JIEDDO. We determined that the data we used were sufficiently reliable for the purpose of this report.

To identify key practices that enabled executing organizations to overcome challenges in the development and fielding of joint urgent needs solutions, we interviewed officials from each initiative and collected data on the challenges that each executing organization encountered. From these interviews, we identified common challenges that initiatives faced—receiving funds and awarding contracts—that could potentially affect the ability of an executing organization to field an urgent capability rapidly. We analyzed how different factors, such as contracting options, affected the time that it took initiatives to reach key events in the urgent needs process. We also reviewed practices that executing organizations employed to overcome these and other programmatic challenges. In performing our work, we obtained documentation to corroborate information provided by officials.

We interviewed officials from the Department of Defense, the Office of the Chairman of the Joint Chiefs of Staff, and the Joint Rapid Acquisition Cell who are responsible for validating and assigning joint urgent needs to military services and other agencies for execution. We also met with officials from Functional Capabilities Boards who were responsible for identifying possible solutions for the urgent needs within our sample. We met with officials from JIEDDO, each military service (Army, Navy, Air Force, and Marine Corps), U.S. Central Command, and Special Operations Command, who were the sponsors responsible for identifying funds and tasking executing organizations or the combatant command that endorsed urgent needs statements.

We conducted this performance audit between January 2011 and April 2012 in accordance with generally accepted government auditing standards. Those standards require that we plan and perform the audit to obtain sufficient, appropriate evidence to provide a reasonable basis for our findings and conclusions based on our audit objectives. We believe that the evidence obtained provides a reasonable basis for our findings and conclusions based on our audit objectives.

Appendix II: Sample Joint Urgent Operational Needs and Executing Organizations

Joint urgent operational need	Executing organization[a]
Afghanistan Counter-Rocket Artillery Mortar	• Army, Counter-Rocket Artillery Mortar Program Directorate
Afghanistan Mine Rollers	• Army, Product Manager Improvised Explosive Device Defeat / Protect Force
All-Terrain Ambulance	• Joint Project Office, Mine Resistant Ambush Protected Vehicle
Enemy Full Motion Video Exploitation	• Intelligence Surveillance Reconnaissance Task Force / Unmanned Aerial Systems Task Force
Handheld Metal Detector	• Army Research Laboratory
Improved Netted Iridium	• Defense Information Systems Agency, Enhanced Mobile Satellite Services Division
Improved Weather Forecasting	• Air Force, Director of Weather
Improved Tactical Handheld Biometrics Solutions	• Army, Program Manager, Biometrics Identity Management Agency
Joint Expeditionary Forensic Facility	• Naval Sea Systems Command, Asymmetric Systems Department
Low and Non-Metallic Buried Improvised Explosive Device Detector	• Army Research Laboratory
Machine Based Language Translation	• Army Research Laboratory
MRAP All-Terrain Vehicle	• Joint Project Office, Mine Resistant Ambush Protected Vehicle
MRAP Wrecker and Tractor	• Joint Project Office, Mine Resistant Ambush Protected Vehicle
National Improvised Explosive Device Exploitation Facility	• Army, Office of the Provost Marshal
Night and All-Weather Counter-Improvised Explosive Device Targeting	• Navy, Space and Naval Warfare Systems Command
Persistent Threat Detection System	• Naval Air Systems Command, Special Surveillance Programs • Army, Project Manager Robotics and Unmanned Systems
Personnel-Borne Improvised Explosive Device / Vehicle-Borne Improvised Explosive Device Detect and Defeat	• Army, Armament Research Development and Engineering Center, Combating Terrorism Technology Team • Army Space & Missile Defense Command / Army Forces Strategic Command • Naval Surface Warfare Center, Directed Energy Warfare Office • Army, Product Manager Improvised Explosive Device Defeat / Protect Force
Real-Time Regional Gateway Integration with Distributed Common Ground System	• Army, Project Manager, Distributed Common Ground System
Robot Repeaters	• Naval Surface Warfare Center, Explosive Ordnance Disposal Technology Division
Stand-Off / Home Made Explosives	• Air Force, Aeronautical Systems Center, Intelligence Surveillance and Surveillance, Sensors • Army Corps of Engineers • Naval Postgraduate School • Army, Night Vision and Electronic Sensors Directorate
Thick Case X-Ray	• Army, Combating Terrorism Technical Support Office • Naval Explosive Ordnance Disposal Technology Division
Unmanned Aerial System Resupply	• Naval Air Systems Command, PMA-266

Joint urgent operational need	Executing organization[a]
Vehicle-Borne Improvised Explosive Device Disruptor	• Department of Energy, Lawrence Livermore National Laboratory
Vehicle Mounted Mine Detection Husky System	• Army, Prototype Integration Facility
Wide-Area Surveillance	• Air Force, Big Safari • Air Force Research Laboratory • Army, Communication-Electronics Research, Development and Engineering Center • Army, Project Manager Robotics and Unmanned Sensors • Army, Project Manager, Airborne Reconnaissance and Exploitation Systems • Army, Project Manager, Unmanned Aerial Systems • Army, Aviation Applied Technology Directorate • Naval Air Systems Command, Special Surveillance Programs • Navy, Wide Focal Plane Array Camera, Integrated Product Team

Source: Department of Defense provided data.

[a]The names of some organizations are not listed because of sensitivity issues.

Appendix III: Comments from the Department of Defense

OFFICE OF THE UNDER SECRETARY OF DEFENSE
3000 DEFENSE PENTAGON
WASHINGTON, DC 20301-3000

ACQUISITION,
TECHNOLOGY
AND LOGISTICS

APR 18 2012

Mr. Michael J. Sullivan
Director, Acquisition and Sourcing Management
U.S. Government Accountability Office
441 G Street, N.W.
Washington, DC 20548

Dear Mr. Sullivan:

This is the Department of Defense (DoD) response to the GAO draft report 12-385, "URGENT WARFIGHTER NEEDS: Opportunities Exist to Expedite Development and Fielding of Joint Capabilities" (GAO Code 120962), dated April 2012. Comments on the report recommendations are enclosed.

The Department expects to complete, in the near future, the report required by section 804 of the Ike Skelton National Defense Authorization Act for Fiscal Year 2011, Section 804, *Review of Acquisition Process for Rapid Fielding of Capabilities in Response to Urgent Operational Needs*. Specific actions accomplished by the Department that relate to the GAO's recommendations also will be included in the report. We anticipate that the report will be delivered to the congressional defense committees in August 2012.

The Department appreciates the opportunity to respond to the draft report. Should you have any questions, please contact Mr. William Beasley, William.Beasley@osd.mil, 703-695-8045.

Sincerely,

Thomas P. Dee
Director, Joint Rapid Acquisition Cell

Enclosure:
As stated

GAO DRAFT REPORT DATED APRIL 2012
GAO-12-385 (GAO CODE 120962)

"URGENT WARFIGHTER NEEDS: OPPORTUNITIES EXIST TO EXPEDITE
DEVELOPMENT AND FIELDING OF JOINT CAPABILITIES"

DEPARTMENT OF DEFENSE COMMENTS
TO THE GAO RECOMMENDATIONS

RECOMMENDATION 1: The GAO recommends that the Secretary of Defense y expedite the
fielding of off-the-shelf solutions by reducing the time it takes to identify the solution and award
a contract.

DoD RESPONSE: Concur. The Department will issue appropriate guidance that will ensure
the urgent needs / rapid acquisition processes meet the warfighter's needs and, when appropriate,
off-the-shelf solutions are identified to resolve an urgent operational need. Additional actions, if
required, to establish mechanisms to ensure off-the-shelf solutions are considered to resolve
urgent operational needs will be addressed in the report required by section 804 of the Ike
Skelton National Defense Authorization Act for Fiscal Year 2011.

RECOMMENDATION 2: The GAO recommends that the Secretary of Defense devise
methods for providing early funding to reimbursable organizations tasked to execute joint urgent
needs.

DoD RESPONSE: Concur. The Department requested and Congress established the Joint
Urgent Operational Need Fund in 10 U.S.C. 2216a, enacted by section 846 of the National
Defense Authorization Act for Fiscal Year 2012, December 31, 2011. Although the President's
budget request for fiscal year 2012 asked for appropriations to the Fund, no funds were
appropriated. The President's budget request for Fiscal Year 2013, includes requests for
appropriations for the Fund. Obtaining this funding is a priority of the Deputy Secretary of
Defense. Additional actions, if required, to establish mechanisms to fund the resolution of
urgent operational needs will be addressed in the report required by section 804 of the Ike
Skelton National Defense Authorization Act for Fiscal Year 2011.

RECOMMENDATION 3: The GAO recommends that the Secretary of Defense
require acquisition organizations to communicate with the combatant commands, such as Central
Command, regularly about progress in executing initiatives and plans for fielding capabilities.

DoD RESPONSE: Concur. In the review required by section 804 of the Ike Skelton National
Defense Authorization Act for Fiscal Year 2011, the end-to-end process will be assessed,
responsibilities defined, and appropriate policy changes initiated. These new policies are
expected to require close interaction with the requesting warfighter to ensure common
understanding on progress and fielding capabilities in response to urgent operational needs.

RECOMMENDATION 4: The GAO recommends that the Secretary of Defense require that an initiative decision memorandum be developed for all initiatives that identifies the acquisition organization responsible for the initiative, schedule estimates, and expectations for acquisition strategies.

DoD RESPONSE: Concur. In the review required by section 804 of the Ike Skelton National Defense Authorization Act for Fiscal Year 2011, the end-to-end process will be assessed, responsibilities defined, and appropriate policy changes initiated. It is expected that additional policy and procedures will require documentation of plans and decisions, commensurate with the urgency of the need. The specific form and timing of such documentation may differ from that recommended by the GAO.

Appendix IV: GAO Contact and Staff Acknowledgments

GAO Contact	Michael Sullivan, (202) 512-4841 or sullivanm@gao.gov
Staff Acknowledgments	Key contributors to this report were Karen Zuckerstein, Assistant Director; James Ashley; Jenny Chanley; Laura Greifner; Melissa Hermes; Laura Jezewski; John Ortiz; Sylvia Schatz; Ryan Stott; Roxanna Sun; and Gavin Ugale.

Related GAO Products

Warfighter Support: DOD's Urgent Needs Processes Need a More Comprehensive Approach and Evaluation for Potential for Consolidation. GAO-11-273. Washington, D.C.: March 1, 2011.

Warfighter Support: Improvements to DOD's Urgent Needs Processes Would Enhance Oversight and Expedite Efforts to Meet Critical Warfighter Needs. GAO-10-460. Washington, D.C.: April 30, 2010.

Warfighter Support: Actions Needed to Improve Visibility and Coordination of DOD's Counter-Improvised Explosive Device Efforts. GAO-10-95. Washington, D.C.: October 29, 2009.

Defense Acquisitions: Rapid Acquisition of MRAP Vehicles. GAO-10-155T. Washington, D.C.: October 8, 2009.

Rapid Acquisition of Mine Resistant Ambush Protected Vehicles. GAO-08-884R. Washington, D.C.: July 15, 2008.

GAO's Mission	The Government Accountability Office, the audit, evaluation, and investigative arm of Congress, exists to support Congress in meeting its constitutional responsibilities and to help improve the performance and accountability of the federal government for the American people. GAO examines the use of public funds; evaluates federal programs and policies; and provides analyses, recommendations, and other assistance to help Congress make informed oversight, policy, and funding decisions. GAO's commitment to good government is reflected in its core values of accountability, integrity, and reliability.
Obtaining Copies of GAO Reports and Testimony	The fastest and easiest way to obtain copies of GAO documents at no cost is through GAO's website (www.gao.gov). Each weekday afternoon, GAO posts on its website newly released reports, testimony, and correspondence. To have GAO e-mail you a list of newly posted products, go to www.gao.gov and select "E-mail Updates."
Order by Phone	The price of each GAO publication reflects GAO's actual cost of production and distribution and depends on the number of pages in the publication and whether the publication is printed in color or black and white. Pricing and ordering information is posted on GAO's website, http://www.gao.gov/ordering.htm. Place orders by calling (202) 512-6000, toll free (866) 801-7077, or TDD (202) 512-2537. Orders may be paid for using American Express, Discover Card, MasterCard, Visa, check, or money order. Call for additional information.
Connect with GAO	Connect with GAO on Facebook, Flickr, Twitter, and YouTube. Subscribe to our RSS Feeds or E-mail Updates. Listen to our Podcasts. Visit GAO on the web at www.gao.gov.
To Report Fraud, Waste, and Abuse in Federal Programs	Contact: Website: www.gao.gov/fraudnet/fraudnet.htm E-mail: fraudnet@gao.gov Automated answering system: (800) 424-5454 or (202) 512-7470
Congressional Relations	Katherine Siggerud, Managing Director, siggerudk@gao.gov, (202) 512-4400, U.S. Government Accountability Office, 441 G Street NW, Room 7125, Washington, DC 20548
Public Affairs	Chuck Young, Managing Director, youngc1@gao.gov, (202) 512-4800 U.S. Government Accountability Office, 441 G Street NW, Room 7149 Washington, DC 20548